Barracks To Boardrooms

Negotiating Your Salary After Serving In The Military

BYRON Y. CHEN

ISBN-10: 1-5188-6227-6
ISBN-13: 978-1-5188622-7-4

Printed in the United States of America.

Ordering Information: Special discounts are available on quantity purchases and purchases made in conjunction with speaking engagements, consulting services, and other in-person events. For details, contact the publisher at the e-mail address Byron@SuccessVets.com.

www.SuccessVets.com

To Mom and Dad.

CONTENTS

INTRODUCTION

WHY DO YOU NEED THIS BOOK?

*"You have to learn the rules of the game.
And then you have to play better than anyone else."*
- Albert Einstein

When it comes to salary negotiation, people don't get what they deserve. People get what they ask for, and most people don't know how to ask. This is the crux of the problem for many employees when they start their new positions at companies.

My first job after leaving the Marine Corps was for a medical device company. I accepted my first offer with elation. Months of networking, interviewing, and refining my resume finally paid off. When I got out of the military, I wondered if I could "make it" in the private sector. I thought that I was going to be working in a meritocracy, where I'd get paid for the value that I brought to a company. And with this first offer, I wondered to myself if I should negotiate it. I reached out to my network of friends and family and they told me, "No, be happy that you got the job." So I didn't. A few months later, I learned what a few of my peers in the industry were earning. That's when I felt duped. They were making so much more. They were doing the same job. They weren't doing it any better or worse than I was. It seemed their salaries had little to do with their technical knowledge or experience. So why the disparity in compensation? I went back to ask my friends and family. Turns out, almost none of them had ever negotiated their salaries before. No wonder they wouldn't recommend that I do it. I dug around for more research and my idea of the private sector being a meritocracy was turned upside down. Companies are not incentivized to pay people beyond what they can get them for. If that is less than market value, all the better. Yet, employers ARE willing to pay more for top quality candidates, IF those candidates negotiate[1]. Most people don't believe this. They think that they do not have the leverage or ability to negotiate. And they end up leaving thousands of dollars on the table that they will never recoup. I want to dispel these fallacies.

Over the next several years, I confided with a veteran hired through the same conference. We got together for lunches and shared the intel we gathered. We were both Marines after all! We found a wide disparity in salaries across the company for the same positions. At first, I thought I couldn't compete with my co-workers. I had just left the Marine Corps. Perhaps my level of skill and experience in my new career wasn't at their level of pay. But after a short time at the company, I knew that wasn't true. That thought is the kind of self-doubt that plagues many employees. I soon realized that what I earned had little to do with experience, skill, or capability. The employees paid the most had demanded compensation packages commensurate with their VALUE. The company didn't just offer it to them. These employees had the skill of negotiation. So I learned how to play the game. Over the rest of my corporate career, I negotiated my salary several times. Each time, I was able to protect my interests while maintaining a good working relationship with my employer. And I increased my earnings every year. I helped many of my family, friends, and other veterans do the same over the years. Even when we couldn't come to terms with an employer, none of us lost our jobs or received demotions. The opposite happened. We were presenting our value to these companies on a consistent basis. Because of that, we were more respected, valued, and received better performance reviews. Even when unsuccessful, negotiating your salary the right way often leads to positive outcomes.

When I transitioned from the Marine Corps, I thought I was ready to take on the world. How hard could the civilian side be? Turns out, it can be pretty frustrating. It's like the rules of "their" society are completely different from the ones that I was used to. In many ways, it's true. There are different experiences and expectations in the civilian world. Before leaving the military, many veterans hold to the belief that they have the skills to do well in the civilian job market. That confidence drops way down after leaving the military[2]. I have felt this myself. I felt overwhelmed by how misunderstood I was as a veteran. Many of my peers faced the same problem. But once I put my efforts into learning the ins and outs of the civilian job market, I succeeded. Many of my friends did the same. What we learned was that we weren't unqualified or unable. We had not practiced many of the skills that were necessary in the job market. Some of these included interviewing, networking, and salary negotiation. The first two skills are important to gain qualified and adequate employment. Salary negotiation is important to ensure satisfaction and self-worth at your job.

Salary negotiation is one of those things that most people are lousy at, not just veterans. I could have written this book for everyone. But I wanted to speak to this current generation of transitioning veterans. I know what they are going through, and I want to address the specific challenges they will face. If you are not a veteran, thank you for picking up this book! I think you will find that the principles and strategies can still be helpful. This book focuses on negotiating your first job offer. Why? Because it's the most important. Your starting salary will be an anchor point that determines your raises and bonuses for your foreseeable career. You don't want to be idle in this. A negotiation is the only way to take action on how much you earn.

Most of the information out there on salary negotiation doesn't paint a true picture of what a battle it can be. What I can offer in the following pages are my lessons learned. I don't like calling myself an expert. I'm a teacher explaining the mechanics of the machine. What you do with the information is all up to you. What's amazing to me is that a negotiation doesn't have to be perfect to work. Most people worry that a negotiation will go wrong and end up hurting their prospects. As you'll learn later in this book, this is rarely the case. What this book will provide you is a set of tactics and principles that you can use to take action the right way. You might only need to use one to negotiate your raise or you might have to use them all. The important lesson is that people don't lose out because they lack leverage. They lose out by not negotiating at all because they think they lack the tools.

Here, are those tools.

CHAPTER ONE

WHY NEGOTIATE YOUR SALARY?

"One of the greatest discoveries a man makes, one of his great surprises,
is to find he can do what he was afraid he couldn't do."
- Henry Ford

The first time I negotiated my salary, I was a mess. My heart was jumping in my throat. My boss had just asked me to move to another city and take on some new responsibilities. It was a good opportunity, especially for someone so new to the industry. But still, I would have to relocate, and I'd be taking on more challenging risks. I already told you how I missed out on negotiating my salary the first time I took a job offer. I had decided that if an opportunity like this came along again, I would leverage the hell out of it. But it felt strange. It felt like I was disagreeing with my father. This was my first boss after the military, and a mentor of mine. He told me what I was going to get paid, and it was better, but not ideal. I had decided that I was going to work on this negotiation, no matter what. As I struggled to keep my voice steady, I said, "I have some concerns with the salary." To my surprise, my boss wasn't outraged, or shocked. He didn't even sound like he cared.

"Yea, OK, of course. Let's make sure this works for you."

Oh, I thought. This isn't so bad after all.

MAKE THOUSANDS OF DOLLARS IN MINUTES WITH THIS ONE LITTLE TRICK

This is the most important chapter of the book. I'm assuming that if you're reading this, you're a capable person. You're competent, perhaps new, but enthusiastic, and definitely a talent worth hiring, or else you wouldn't need to read this book. But you're not sure if you're getting an offer that you deserve. Don't worry, because you're not alone.

Most people do not negotiate their starting salaries or compensation packages with their employers. I'm sure you can infer this, or confirm it by asking a few of your friends, but you can also check the research:

1. A 2013 CareerBuilder survey[1] showed that 49% of workers accepted the first offer given to them, even though 45% of employers responding said they were willing and expected a salary negotiation. Even if employers were unwilling to adjust salaries, 62% were willing to compromise on other areas such as vacation time and expenses.

2. In 2012, Salary.com published an article showing that employees negotiating initial offers had declined by 6% and that 41% did not negotiate salary for the job they currently hold[2].

3. In an infographic of over 800 people surveyed by Salary.com[3], 86% of employees wanted to learn how to negotiate more effectively. Yet, 26% did not know the industry standard for their position's salary. And only 11% were satisfied with their original offer. What happened with everyone else? They attributed not negotiating to lack of confidence, lack of skill, or finding negotiation unpleasant.

4. In a research study titled, "Women Don't Ask," the gender wage gap between women and men is found to be at least partially attributed to women being less likely to negotiate their salaries[4]. This has negatively affected women's earnings over the long term.

To summarize the results of those studies, not enough people negotiate when they can, and should, do so. And why don't more people try to negotiate? The most popular answer was that they didn't know how. The second most popular answer was that they felt uncomfortable asking. It's quite understandable. Most people just aren't well versed in handling a negotiation. We are also taught to avoid conflict from a young age, and negotiation just feels…not right.

So if there is only one thing I convince you to do in this book, it would be to JUST ASK for more when you get offered a job. If you can find it within yourself to JUST ASK, you will have gotten farther along than many people out there in the workforce (suckers…OK, not really, just uninformed or unconfident). The rest of this book will dive into strategies and tactics, but it all boils down to one thing. JUST ASK. It might feel uncomfortable. You will feel unprepared. And you'll be OK.

Negotiating your initial salary will put you in control of your career. Here are more reasons why you need to do it.

YOUR RECRUITER WILL NOT DO IT FOR YOU

The only person who will want to negotiate your salary is you. If you, like many transitioning veterans, work with a recruiter to get your job, you might assume that he will work to get you your highest salary. It would be reasonable to assume this, since many times, the recruiter's commission is based on the salary you receive from the employer. But the incentives for recruiters to get the highest possible offer for you are not aligned with yours. The authors of the book *Freakonomics* detail a similar relationship between home owners and their real estate agents[5]. Studies showed that real estate agents, on average, accepted lower offers for their clients compared to when agents sold their own properties. This is because the extra effort required for agents to sell someone else's home does not result in a significant enough difference in commission to do so. After all, they only make a percentage of the deal. That extra effort isn't worth it if they can make more by closing more deals. In no way am I saying that recruiters or real estate agents are being dishonest. But realize that you have much more at stake when it comes to negotiating a salary offer than the person working as your agent. If you have a recruiter as a buffer, you have to push him to get the best offer for you.

TRAINING YOUR EMPLOYER

The more often you negotiate with someone, the more likely that person is to negotiate with you in the future. Makes sense right? If you find a car salesman you find to be fair, wouldn't you keep buying cars from her in the future? The same goes for salary negotiations, because this won't be the last one in your career. You want to get your employer used to you asking for raises. This may be subconscious, but they will be more willing to deal with you over time. If you ask for your first raise 15 years into your career, they will find it shocking. If you get in the habit of asking for one every year, not so shocking. In fact, you should get in the habit of doing this frequently. But it all starts with the initial one.

THERE IS NO BETTER TIME THAN NOW

You will rarely be in a better bargaining position, both on paper, and in the mind of your employer, than at the moment they've decided that they want to hire you. This is where their desire to "get you" is strongest. And in fact, it will diminish immediately after they've brought you on. Raises nowadays barely outpace inflation. If you don't start negotiating immediately, don't place your bets on getting recognized for your value to your company down the road.

DISPROPORTIONATE EFFECTS

The most important reason to negotiate your first offer is to look at the opportunity cost of not negotiating. Your initial salary will be the basis for all future bonuses, increases, and negotiations. When you look at the math over the long term, one could argue that in a worst case scenario where a company retracted its offer and you had to spend a few months to find another job but could negotiate a better starting salary, you would be better off.

"Not negotiating, however, can be more costly than you think. In their paper 'Who Asks and Who Receives in Salary Negotiation,' researchers Michelle Marks and Crystal Harold found that employees who negotiated their salary boosted their annual pay on average of $5,000. According to the researchers, assuming a 5% average annual pay increase over a 40-year career, a 25-year-old who negotiated a starting salary of $55,000 will earn $634,000 more than a non-negotiator who accepted an initial offer of $50,000."[6]
- Camille Sweeney and Josh Gosfield in Fast Company, 2013

Imagine that. Over a half a million dollars in your lifetime by doing this one little thing. JUST ASK.

SUMMARY

- Most people don't negotiate their starting salaries, even though employers often have wiggle room in their offer and may even be expecting a counter.
- You are in control of the process. Do not count on someone else to negotiate for you.
- The potential long term benefits of negotiating greatly outweigh the negative consequences in most cases.
- Merely asking for more puts you in a better position than most people who go through the hiring process. So just do it.

CHAPTER TWO

STRATEGIES FOR TAKING ACTION

"I shall proceed from the simple to the complex. But in war more than in any other subject we must begin by looking at the nature of the whole; for here more than elsewhere the part and the whole must always be thought of together"
- Carl von Clausewitz

You know that every battle is different. When you first start training in the military you learn tactics. Tactics are simple. Logical. *Executable*. But you don't win wars on tactics alone. You can know every tactic out there, but the other side can and will change it on you. So you must know common tactics, but you must also be ready to make your own. This book follows the timeline of a salary negotiation, from preparation to acceptance. But in reality, there is no Step 1 through Step 5 for negotiation success. The process will be fluid. You will have to adapt.

I've covered as many tactics as I can in this book, without writing *War And Peace*. In order to adapt to tactics that may not be covered in this book, you have to understand strategy. The following are characteristics common to every salary negotiation. Understanding these characteristics will help you put together a strategy for any situation.

PREPARATION

There are two aspects to preparation in a salary negotiation. First, is your understanding of the landscape in which you are negotiating. What sets many people back when they accept a job offer is that they have no idea if the offer is a good one or not. Don't make this mistake. You have no excuse to not know what the range of compensation is for the position. This book will teach you what information you need and how to find it. You can't argue for more if you don't know if more is reasonable.

The other aspect of preparation is personal. Have you practiced the ability to communicate your value and then to ask for it in a professional way? Most people are afraid to negotiate because they feel that they lack the skills. Of course they do. They don't negotiate enough to develop any skills. You must practice the elements of a negotiation, even if it's just acting it out with a partner. You have to consider what makes your position stronger, how to weave it into the conversation, and how to demonstrate confidence in it. You have to prepare.

COMMUNICATE VALUE

Throughout the interview, you are looking to demonstrate that you will have a positive impact at the company. Some of this value is determined intrinsically. You are valued because you would be a good fit with the culture of the company. So make sure you highlight how good of a fit you are with the company during the interview process. Extrinsically, your value is determined by the market, how much you can make for the company, or how much money you can save the company.

To communicate value throughout the process, you want to relate how your background and skills put you at the upper end of talent that is available on the market. As a veteran, you have a key advantage here. Your time in the military has given you experiences with a wide variety of skills and situations that have relevance in the corporate world. This is not always apparent because of the difference in lingo and lack of understanding on the civilian side. While a common complaint amongst veterans, you must learn to overcome this. Educate yourself on business terms and find similarities in the position with what you did in the military. Talk about your background in those terms. For example, an employer may be looking for someone who can manage technical projects with diverse teams. I'm willing to bet that many veterans can provide examples of times they've worked with technical projects such as managing electronics equipment, vehicles, weapons, even computer systems, all while collaborating with different agencies and personnel. This is something that can set you apart from other candidates. Your communications strategy in salary negotiations is to identify what is valuable to your potential employer and relating how your skills or experiences fit the position in jargon they understand.

THINK COLLABORATION, NOT CONFLICT

While I may talk about negotiation in terms of battle and conflict, a salary negotiation is ultimately about collaboration. You want something. The employer wants you. You just don't agree on the price for the exchange of your services. You are looking for ways to solve this problem with your employer. Taking a combative tone will most likely not benefit you in a salary negotiation. If this were a negotiation to get a good deal on a car, you could make the salesperson angry and just walk away and find another dealership. If this is a job that you really want, then you have to consider the consequences. Throughout the salary negotiation, think about it from your employer's perspective. Why are they trying to hire you? How can you help them? What do you need to demonstrate to prove that you are worthy of higher compensation? Figure out how to solve their problems and it will benefit you.

MANAGE TENSION

Most people are not comfortable with saying, "No," or making demands, especially when it comes to their potential employer. To get what you are worth, you will have to stand your ground and be confident in your preparation and understanding of what value you bring. If you are working with someone who is skilled at negotiation, they will parry your first attempt, perhaps even try to bully you down from your position. You have to gauge when you should push back, and when you should bend. This is something that can be tough to do. My general rule: be aggressive in your strategy, and conciliatory in your tone.

You might have to say something like, "I don't mean to be difficult as I am truly enthusiastic about this offer. I just believe that my experiences and skills bear a higher salary than what you have offered, considering all the research I have done on the industry. Perhaps we can go over my research to help me understand where I can add value to the company and work on a compensation package that is fair to both of us." The translation for this is, "Don't be cheap because I'm worth more than what you are offering. Let me explain why and then to save face for you, I'll say we are working on a solution together." See how the first one sounds nicer, but you're pushing for the same thing as the second statement? Just imagine smoothing things over with your NCO or commander. You get the idea.

Now that you understand the strategy of negotiations, you can adapt variations of tactics from this book to fit your situation. As you continue to read, feel free to skip to different chapters to focus on your areas of weakness. Perhaps you are a confident individual. You are ready to negotiate your salary, right now. In that case, you might not need to read the chapter on mindset. Figure out where you need help and read the chapter to work on that. You can also look further into the studies and articles I reference throughout the book. The notes to find them are collected together for this purpose under *Endnotes*.

SUMMARY

• You will not be able to learn and anticipate every negotiation tactic. Understand the strategy behind negotiation to be able to adapt to any situation.

• Salary negotiations require you to prepare, communicate your value, collaborate, and manage tension throughout the process.

• Focus on your strengths and shore up your weaknesses with further research and practice.

CHAPTER THREE

MINDSET FOR SUCCESS

"If you imagine less, less will be what you undoubtedly deserve."
- Debbie Millman, American writer and designer

Your mindset is just as important to a successful salary negotiation as anything else. When I was getting ready to go to the Naval Academy, I would practice for their physical fitness test. I had gotten 87 pushups out of a maximum possible of 101. I thought I did pretty well. That was the kind of person I was at the time. I wanted to do "pretty well" in everything. I thought 87 was a pretty good number. When I showed up for the first day of training and ran the tests, there were students around me who all hit the 101 mark. I felt a bit sheepish. My expectations for myself quickly changed. And the following week, I tested out at 101, as well. You see, the problem with me wasn't ability. I had let myself believe that I had achieved what I could, and that limited what I could actually do. Salary negotiation is no different. Whenever I broach the subject with people, more often than not, I get excuses – not reasons – why they just cannot negotiate.

We frequently prevent ourselves from fulfilling our full potential. The self-doubts that hold us back from doing what we can are called limiting beliefs.

"A limiting belief is something that you believe about yourself, other people, or the world – and although it isn't actually true, the fact that you think it is holds

you back from experience and success. Any time you tell yourself you "can't" do something that's within the realm of human possibility – that's a limiting belief."
- Neil Strauss in Rules of the Game

If you don't have any mental hang-ups before your negotiation, you can skip this chapter. That means you have a healthy confidence and understanding of your value, and you are able to communicate this in your body language and conversation. If it's a belief that is holding you back from negotiating your salary, it is important to confront it and evaluate whether or not that belief is true. You still might be insecure after your realize what's holding you back, but at least then, you understand why and can work to move past it.

Read through the following examples of common limiting beliefs. Are any of them things that you believe? I will try to dispel these myths to help you overcome them.

IF I TRY TO NEGOTIATE, I WILL LOSE THE JOB OFFER

Unless it's a job that they gave you just because you have a heartbeat, then you have some skills that make you talented and unique. I'll talk more about which jobs are better for negotiating salaries later, but let's assume it took some time and effort to recruit you to the point that the company is offering you a job. Do you know what the cost is of finding talent these days? A 2013 Deloitte study showed that U.S. companies spent over $72 BILLION to recruit employees[1]. That's over $3,300 dollars spent to find and vet someone. That is pricey, and the more skill a position requires, the higher that number goes. When a company finds the right person, they do not want to lose that person over a salary negotiation. Furthermore, a company that does renege on an offer because you want to negotiate it, likely has other issues you would not want to deal with by working there.

I SHOULD BE HAPPY WITH A JOB IN THIS ECONOMY

You might think that employers have all the power in hiring, but that's just not true. In 2013, there were reportedly 11 million unemployed Americans. Yet, employers reported 4 million jobs that had to be filled[2]. Companies are desperate to find top quality employees, but due to recruiting inefficiencies, it's still tough, even in today's market, to find the right person for the job. How valuable do you think you are then, when a company figures out YOU are the right person for the job? Companies should be just as happy finding YOU in this economy, as you are of finding them.

I DON'T DESERVE IT BECAUSE I'M NEW/OLD/JUST STARTING OUT/GRADUATING/COMING FROM A DIFFERENT INDUSTRY

This is bullshit. Your value as an employee does not come from any of these qualities. You might have to fight some assumptions to be able to negotiate your salary higher. But what this book will teach is that leverage comes from perceived VALUE. Get out of the mindset that you have to "earn your bones" or work your way up the ladder. If you can demonstrate the immense value that you will be providing an employer, they will want to incentivize you to work for them.

I DON'T WANT TO ANNOY PEOPLE

Umm...get over it. OK, I get it. It's uncomfortable. But why would you assume that you are going to annoy someone else by asking a reasonable question? Think of it this way. The company hiring you wants to get the best deal possible. They are not going to hesitate to offer less than market value or what you may actually deserve. It's your responsibility, nay duty, to ask for what's yours. If you do so professionally, courteously, and reasonably, there is no reason for your employers to be offended. Now, not everyone can be expected to be reasonable, but that's not your problem. And wouldn't you want to find that out when discussing the value that you bring, rather than later on when you are working for the company, and cannot bring up critical issues because "people will get annoyed?" You may ruffle a few feathers, but as I mentioned before, the consequences are not that dire if you do. And from this book, you'll learn to negotiate in such a way that you will not be seen as an annoyance. If you can't defend your value here, how are you going to defend yourself with anything else at your new job? Control what you can control. It's true, some people might be offended if you try to negotiate. People are also offended that you served your country, or put baby pictures on Facebook, or went to the concert they couldn't go to. Do you let these things control your life? Focus on what you can control...your ability to negotiate your salary.

MY JOB DOESN'T ALLOW IT

Who says? Did everyone else you talk to say it? Did they actually ask and try? Just because someone doesn't expect you to negotiate doesn't mean you can't. Most employers are willing to negotiate salary, and even more are willing to negotiate other aspects of the compensation package like time off, expenses, and telecommuting[3]. You can always ask, and the answer might be, "No," but you haven't violated any laws or broken the universe by doing so.

I CAN PROVE MYSELF AT THE JOB AND THE COMPANY WILL GIVE ME A RAISE LATER

Many people talk themselves into waiting a few months, years, or decades and using this time to prove themselves before asking for a salary increase, if at all. Or they expect that their company will adequately evaluate their contribution. Understand this – you have little control over the future. Your best time to make demands is now. You will see in later chapters that you currently have a great deal of leverage. You want to use this leverage because you may not have it later or it may not be as strong. There's nothing wrong with demanding to be paid for your performance beforehand. Getting a higher salary is not likely to make you "more fire-able" in the future. You can either do a good job or not. Getting paid more for it now means less aggravation for you than if you have to negotiate it later.

I DON'T THINK I'M WORTH THIS MUCH

What is value? Negotiation is about making your value apparent and getting a fair exchange for it. Do you know how much you're worth? Have you done the research into what is comparable in the industry? Have you done the math to find out how much money your efforts can make or save for the company? This is your actual value – not what you perceive it to be.

I'M NOT A GOOD NEGOTIATOR/COMMUNICATOR/SPEAKER

Very few people are naturally good at it. But it can be learned. Even people who seem adept at negotiation without prior training probably had life experiences that taught them the concepts that they now do unconsciously. You can learn. You have to practice. And you can get good at it.

PERHAPS YOU HAVE SOME DOUBTS THAT I DIDN'T COVER

It's OK to have doubts. It's important to evaluate these thoughts to see if they hold true and are helpful or hurtful to your current situation. You didn't prepare yourself to go into battle without pushing out the doubts that crept up in your head. It's important to evaluate your thoughts like these. Are they ACTUALLY true? Many successful people have doubts. But in the face of those doubts, they persevere.

OVERCOMING LIMITING BELIEFS

The next step in dispelling limiting beliefs is to pattern a new way of thinking that is healthier. You've identified and become aware of thoughts that are holding you back. Now you have to develop new thoughts that support what you are trying to accomplish. For each limiting belief that you have, come up with a new choice. This new choice should empower you, not discourage you. Let's take one example from above.

I am the type of person who doesn't want to annoy people. This was a major concern for me when I negotiated my salary. I was able to recognize this, and replace it with something more helpful. Instead of thinking that I might annoy people when negotiating, I think:

I am a professional. I cannot control how other people will react. But I will conduct myself with integrity, honesty, and professionalism. I am not being annoying. I am acting reasonably and straightforwardly.

This is an exercise that you have to do consistently to overcome limiting beliefs. Remember, your beliefs stem from experiences and lessons throughout your life. It can take a great deal of work to overcome what holds you back internally. I'm not going to tell you to write these things down and repeat them to yourself every morning and to dance under a bright moon to fix your mental game. Recognize what's holding you back and change it. There are people that have written about this sort of self-development far better than I could. If you're looking for more help with this, I suggest checking out Tony Robbins' book *Awaken The Giant Within*.

It might seem like a hokey exercise to alter your beliefs before taking action in your life. But this is the same formula the military uses to train its troops. When you get to boot camp, the goal is to break you down and build up your beliefs system from the ground up – everything from how you tie your shoes to how to conduct yourself. Regardless of your military specialty, these overarching core beliefs are what impel you to act the way you should in uniform. Your beliefs system has a similarly profound effect on you, even when you don't put on a uniform.

SUMMARY

- Evaluate your beliefs for any negative associations with negotiating your salary.
- Confront these beliefs and assess whether they are actually true, or limitations you are placing on yourself.
- Supplant your limiting beliefs with empowering beliefs.

CHAPTER FOUR

IS THIS NEGOTIABLE?

"Let us never negotiate out of fear. But let us never fear to negotiate."
- John F. Kennedy

When I was a company commander in the Marine Corps, my job included overseeing training exercises for my Marines. Part of the planning included requesting resources from various departments for things like food, bullets, equipment, and even permits for where and when we could blow stuff up. All of these things, of course, are governed by departments with their own strict rules and regulations to follow. Every once in a while, something would get denied for a dumb reason. Some piece of paperwork wasn't e-mailed to the right person, or I pissed off some staff officer, or the Private First Class receiving the request moved it into his inbox which doubles as a trash can. In cases like this, some might point to the rules and regulations and think, well, we are out of luck. But there is always a human being who ultimately makes the decision on rules and regulations. I would bring my staff in and say, "All right, let's figure out who I need to buy a case of beer to make this happen." Now I didn't always have to shell out a bribe to get things to happen. Often it would just take someone from my staff to go and explain to their counterparts what the situation was and a compromise would be made. My point is, even in the strict world of the military, there's always room to negotiate.

I suspect that one of the reasons people don't negotiate is that they don't know if it's appropriate. And most people err on the side of caution. So they don't ask. You've already learned why it rarely hurts to ask. But that doesn't mean that your negotiation will be successful. It is important to figure out the strength of your starting position. The position itself is not the only factor that goes into your leverage, of course. We'll get to this in later chapters, but as an example, if a company says it's their policy not to negotiate, and you have three better offers to consider, you could use this as leverage to get them to make an exception to their policy. But understanding your starting position is important because it informs you of how much leverage you have in the negotiation. Weak position = less leverage. On the other hand, it should boost your confidence if your situation starts off in a strong position.

Let's take a look at some of the characteristics of different positions that make it harder to negotiate.

LOW WAGE JOBS
The lower the wage that the job starts at, the less easy it will be to negotiate. Partly this is because there isn't much room to move the needle. Going from $10 to $15 an hour is just too big of a percentage jump to negotiate unless other factors are involved. You can also assume that the reason wages for this job are low is because it includes some combination of the other characteristics listed below that give the position a poor starting position in negotiation.

LOW DEMAND SKILLS
If the job you are pursuing is easily done by many people, you may not have the leverage to negotiate. Any extra skills that you bring from your background just don't have any relevance in many cases like this. You don't need any leadership experience to flip burgers. The more likely that the job can be performed consistently and competently by other people, the less likely you have any value to add that will lead to a salary increase.

HIGH SUPPLY
This one is not as difficult to negotiate around, depending on the skill level required. High supply means, of course, that a company has

many options in the candidate pool. High supply does not necessarily mean that you are out of luck though. Some high turnover jobs in consulting and sales fields are always looking to attract talented individuals. The interview process up to the point where you receive an offer may be highly competitive for jobs like these, and you may want to be extra cautious not to divulge that you plan on playing hardball with the salary. While a lot of people may be able to fill the job offering, these companies may need to throw in incentives to entice people to stay.

HIGHLY STRUCTURED INDUSTRIES

You know from the military that some salaries are set. Some contracting jobs and government jobs are like this. Or perhaps the union sets the standards of pay. This doesn't mean you are completely out of luck. But it will be difficult. Your options for this may be to negotiate to enter in at a higher position, or to accelerate your review or promotion period. Just understand that the salary itself may be set for whatever position you take.

ENTRY LEVEL/CERTIFICATIONS/REQUIRED YEAR'S EXPERIENCE

Some jobs require certain certifications or years of experience for you to get a certain salary. Or the company only allows you to enter the entry level position, which has a fixed salary. If you have the skills, but are missing the official qualifications, the obstacle in these cases is that you have to convince your employer that you are qualified and deserve a different starting salary. Or it means that you may not be able to negotiate your starting salary, but perhaps there is room to negotiate your starting position.

When you face a situation where the job you are applying for falls under any of the above characteristics, what do you do? Well, like I said at the start of the chapter, it never hurts to ask. Set your expectations low. Once you've received the offer, a simple request on whether or not there is leeway in their offer might be all the effort you put forth. You might still be surprised with a yes, and you risk little in asking.

Now let's take a look at some characteristics of positions where it may be easier to negotiate.

LONG AND INVOLVED INTERVIEW PROCESS

The more a company spends recruiting you, the more you can be assured that the salary is negotiable. Did the process involve meeting with several managers, travel accommodations, and comped meals? Did you interview over several rounds? Did you meet with several members of the team, all or most of whom have a say in your hiring? Understand that these incur costs in time and money for the company. You don't spend thousands of dollars recruiting someone just to short them a few thousand on the backend when you finally find the person you want. At the end of all this, if the company gives you an offer, you can be pretty confident that you've got room to negotiate.

JOBS WITH SPECIAL RISKS

Risks can include danger to life, like in some oil and gas job fields, or risk to career, like a startup. If there are things about the job that equally talented individuals would not take, then you may have room to negotiate. What if the job is located in a less than desirable place to live? If it's a tough field to attract the right talent, then there are probably some things you can ask for in return.

CURRENT EMPLOYEES HAVE A RANGE OF SALARIES

Compare the salaries of employees in the industry, or with the same position in the company itself. If there is a range, then you can probably make a case for what your salary deserves to be. I talk later about how to find this information out. What is important is knowing whether or not these salaries are different for reasons based on the individual, or the region. For example, salaries might be different based on cost of living differences between locations. However, if salaries vary in the same location, then it is likely that you have room to negotiate.

IF YOU HAVE MULTIPLE OFFERS

If you're in a situation where you have multiple offers, then you have an opportunity to play these off each other. There are, of course, considerations for you when making this decision. Perhaps the company with the job you want most just won't raise their offer. You'll have to consider your priorities, but you give yourself the ability to negotiate by having other options.

In the end, there are a wide range of jobs that fall on the obvious ends of the spectrum with another bunch in the ambiguous pile when determining their negotiating positions. But like I said at the start of this chapter, if there's a human being behind the decision, there is always room to negotiate. Compare which of the characteristics describe the position you are going after to assess how much leverage you have. Understanding your starting position is key to your negotiation strategy, including what you counter with and how long you hold out.

SUMMARY

• Consider local market demand, skill set, risks, and what you observe throughout the interview process when considering if the job will be negotiable.

• The more characteristics in your favor means that you have greater leverage to use in negotiating.

• The more leverage you have, the stronger your negotiation position should be. If you're in a poor starting position, set your expectations low. If your starting position is strong, put forth the effort to prepare a strong counter.

CHAPTER FIVE

WHAT GOES INTO YOUR COMPENSATION?

"If you are good at something, never do it for free."
- The Joker, from The Dark Night

A lot of people miss the opportunity to negotiate their salaries because they fail to realize all the different options that are up for negotiation. Being a good negotiator means understanding all the options available to you, and being able to leverage these things to your advantage. It's quite possible that your company will not budge on your base salary. That doesn't mean that you should give up once you learn this. There are many areas that the company may be willing to be flexible.

So what goes into your compensation and what affects it? We'll go into each of the terms and factors along with discussing how they can impact your negotiations. This is a starting point. I suggest that if you see any of the following or anything that's not mentioned in an offer, do further research.

BASE SALARY

For some positions, this may be the only value associated with your compensation. Your base salary isn't just dreamed up by your company. It could be influenced by where you work, the industry you're in, how much experience you have, and how the company is doing. Understanding this gives you a better idea if you can negotiate this number. For example, poor economy, low income area, dying industry – all would lead to the conclusion that the base salary is probably set. On the other hand, if you have in-demand skills in a high cost of living area with a quick growing company, you may be able to negotiate a top of the industry salary.

RETIREMENT

What retirement benefits does the company offer? This is definitely something that you want to compare across industries and companies. You'll be surprised at how generous some companies are, while others are very stingy. It's easy to forget about considering this because it usually requires you to do research on the plan itself, and may not be apparent in the offer contract. For example, your company may have a 401k plan that includes matching percentages depending on how much of your salary you contribute. This percentage varies widely, and could be a difference of thousands of dollars per year. Make sure you use this to assess the offers given to you, and to point these out if they work to your advantage as a point of leverage in the negotiation.

HEALTH INSURANCE

Different health insurance providers cover different costs. If your company provides health insurance that will reimburse the price tag for your child's braces, this could be additional thousands of dollars to your bottom line. This is a variable that can be very different from individual to individual, so it's important to consider for yourself if you can take advantage of the health coverage from your company. For example, my company's insurance plan covered up to 16 chiropractic visits a year. I took advantage of this fully, which totaled nearly $1,200 in additional benefits. But what if I was never going to use these benefits? Some companies tout their strong health plan as a huge benefit, but if it's not something that you will be likely to take advantage of, perhaps you can negotiate to lower your plan coverage, or just point out that it is not of interest to you and you need other things to entice you.

COMMISSION

Commission is included for many sales positions. Some are on a sliding scale, increasing as you bring in more volume or higher priced sales. These scales or the starting commission itself may be negotiable. This is a great negotiation point because you only get paid if you are making money for the company. The best source of information from this will be from people in the industry. I'll talk more about this research in the next chapter.

VESTING

Some bonuses or options are tied to a commitment for length of time that you work with the company. It's important to understand this since a $10,000 signing bonus may not be as attractive if it's tied to a five year vesting period. That means if you leave before the end of five years, you could be on the hook to return some or the entire bonus. Be sure to divide the bonus or value of the options by the vesting period to see its value year over year. If you don't expect other increases in compensation or salary over that time, then that money spread over all those years might not be worth what you could get in a different company with normal salary raises. Employers may entice you with a big number up front to lock you in over several years. On a side note, some anecdotal evidence has shown me that it may be tough for your employer to try to recover this money from you. It's not exactly like the military where they can just take this amount from your paycheck. They may not put in the effort and cost in trying to recover this bonus if you leave. Still, that's a risk you'll have to consider.

OPTIONS AND STOCK

Some companies may provide stock or options to their employees. There are different kinds of stock and their value can vary wildly, even within the same company. Stocks and options are also often tied to a vesting period, as mentioned above, so you may not receive some or all of the equity until you have worked beyond a certain period of time. You will want to look into the specifics of this and compare to what is generally offered in the industry, as well as to other employees.

EXPENSES

Some companies provide expense accounts. These expenses may cover everything from your office to driving costs. While a variable savings, you can talk to others in the company to see how much you end up getting reimbursed with the expense account. It's also important to understand how it works. Do you have to pay out of pocket and submit them for approval to HR? How are items tracked? One good example is mileage for travel. At my previous company, we were given $0.25 per mile for business travel with our personal vehicles. This was in contrast to other companies that provided a charge card for gas fill-ups. This could impact your bottom-line, and should factor in to your consideration of the overall compensation package.

VACATION AND SICK DAYS

How many of these do you get? Do they rollover each year? Do they pay you for them if you leave the company? What if you're laid off? Companies have been known to not pay these off if you don't use them. You might think, I'll just make sure I use them all. Is the company's operating tempo going to allow you to take two straight weeks off? Not always. Can you negotiate more days off? Beyond figuring out how much it adds to your bottom line, you need to calculate how important this benefit is to your quality of life.

WORKING FROM HOME OR TELECOMMUTING

People sometimes neglect to take into account the freedom and control one has when working from home. It can be a great luxury. Is this an option for you? If you need a flexible schedule, this could be a worthwhile trade in negotiation. In some companies, this might be a great leverage point, as it could lower their costs, as well.

SCHOOL, CERTIFICATIONS, AND TUITION

Does the company pay for additional schools or pay off loans? These costs can wipe out debt or greatly increase your future earnings value. If they have programs like these, can you take advantage of them? It's a perk not everyone will use, so if the company offers it you have to consider if it's a worthwhile addition for you in your compensation package.

RELOCATION

Moving around in the military is a hassle, but the military covers these costs. Will the company offer the same for you if you have to relocate? This can be worth thousands. Remember, don't do anything as a favor to the company if you can get it paid for. Relocation is a good leverage point in negotiations because it can be a reasonable one-off cost for the company as part of hiring you. Your employer may be more willing to consider negotiating this than other parts of your salary that will impact them long term.

JOB TITLE

Job title might be something you can easily negotiate at no cost to the company. Why would this be important? Beyond pride, think about your future. If you can get a job title upgrade, it may equate to better opportunities in the future at other companies. Sometimes, a senior title is associated with automatic raises in compensation. Maybe it puts you on a fast track for promotion. Consider the long term effects of a title upgrade. Some promotions at work are not available unless you're in a certain position for a certain amount of time. Don't underestimate the value of time acceleration to your career.

ACCELERATED REVIEW PERIODS

Review periods are often associated with pay raises and bonuses. Negotiating accelerated reviews means you can move up the chain faster, or get a raise sooner. For some companies, negotiations only take place after review periods. Why wait a whole year to discuss this when you are performing at that level six months in? If you can work at a level that merits recognition, look at shortening review periods as a possible way to accelerate your earnings.

NON-COMPETE CLAUSES

For some industries, competitors poaching employees is a major issue. Companies may try to prevent this by putting a clause in your contract that prevents you from working for a competitor for a certain amount of time. This could diminish your ability to move to other positions. Perhaps getting this removed from your contract would be beneficial to your long term goals. Or in exchange for committing to such a clause, you require a higher salary to hedge against the prospects of going to the competitor.

SEVERANCE

Sometimes, companies will lay out severance packages in the compensation package. This means if you are laid off, they provide a set salary, vacation payback, etc. Even if this doesn't come into play, it's important to remember to look at this as a possible thing to negotiate. You never know when you might get let go. Make sure that if this is part of the contract, there is enough of a runway for you to take care of yourself and your family.

TERM AND TERMINATION

Let me compare this to the different contracts and options that the military offers. For example, you could be a reservist on a one year active reserve tour, or you re-enlist for a four year option in a certain occupational specialty. In the public sector, there are many types of employment contracts. You could be employed "at will" meaning you could be terminated at any time. Or perhaps you have an employment contract, meaning you are obligated to stay through the contract period. The contract may even lay out under what circumstances you may be terminated. Is there a probationary period when you may be evaluated more frequently or paid differently? These things get very particular to the company, so it is important to understand all aspects of this before your sign on. Make sure to bring up any questions and ask if they offer different terms if it is not clear whether or not this is something you can negotiate.

There's an unlimited number of things that you can negotiate in your compensation package. The ones listed are the common ones. But you can get creative with it. I've known people who have negotiated getting gift cards and other quirky items in their contract. What's important is that you understand what goes into your contract and to work with your employer to evaluate if there is a fairer option for you.

SUMMARY

• Consider the total compensation package when evaluating an offer. Make sure you understand all aspects of the contract.
• Figure out what is of benefit TO YOU. If you're not going to take advantage of a certain benefit, see if it is negotiable or use it as a leverage point to get what you do want.

- Compare each part of the offer across similar industries, companies, and positions to see if the compensation is better or worse than what you could get, elsewhere. Use the differences as leverage in your negotiation.

CHAPTER SIX

RESEARCHING SALARY

"The commander must decide how he will fight the battle before it begins. He must then decide how he will use the military effort at his disposal to force the battle to swing the way he wishes it to go; he must make the enemy dance to his tune from the beginning and not vice versa."
- Field Marshall Bernard Montgomery

Research is critical to a successful salary negotiation. Employers know that they must provide competitive salaries to attract the best talent. Your research will give you an idea of how much room you have to negotiate and what you may be able to leverage.

Your main goal is to figure out what the market rate is for the position that you are going after. Market rate is fluid and flexible. Whatever range you find out will not be the exact range that you are negotiating against. After all, your company may assess things differently or the data you find may be old. Your research will help you gauge the initial offer and form your counter.

INDUSTRY AND POSITION

Nowadays, online research allows for easy access to broad job market data. You can look at sites like Glassdoor.com, Monster.com, Salaryexpert.com, or Salary.com for company reviews and income information. You can get an idea of how salaries compare for the same position across the industry and different companies.

COST OF LIVING

Cost of living factors like housing, utilities, and transportation can influence the value of your salary. Calculators can be found online at Bestplaces.net/cost-of-living, Numbeo.com/cost-of-living, or Money.cnn.com/calculator/pf/cost-of-living to compare the buying power of salaries in different places. Careeronestop.org has a search function that allows you to get salary ranges for occupations differentiated by location.

You will also have to assign an internal value for things that won't come up in a compensation package. Do you prefer cities to rural towns? Is school district important to you? In what part of the country do you want to live? This is difficult to put a dollar amount on, but you should ask yourself, "How much would it be worth to me not to get my preferences?" And vice versa.

COMPANY FACTORS

Beyond salary information, you want to figure out if the company culture matches your own. Glassdoor.com, as mentioned before, may be a good place to find out more about the company. Be wary though, as the site is meant to be a place for people to anonymously review their employers. Like anything on the internet, this can be severely biased. Take the information with a grain of salt, and the more reviews, the better. Your research into the company should also include the company's market cap, revenues, stage of growth, and other financial factors. All of these can influence how the company compensates their employees. If it is a public company, you can find that information at Finance.yahoo.com. For private companies, look for industry sites or news articles that report this information. These are also questions you can ask your recruiter during the interview process. Understanding the financial health of a company helps you gauge whether or not it can make an offer in line with the rest of the industry.

If an employer has sponsored visas to hire foreign employees, the company is required to report certain information, including the wages for a position. You can use this to get a range for salaries at that position. This information is available at Visadoor.com.

NETWORKING

Do some networking and gather human intelligence. Use LinkedIn to find veterans or other people you have some sort of connection to who can tell you more about the position, the company, or the industry. Be wary when reaching out to current employees. Keep the discussion professional and don't push hard on the questions about salary until you know it's someone you can trust. This person can always talk to the people in the hiring process, so you want to make sure their impression of you is a good one. Some employees may also be governed by a non-disclosure agreement, so it might not even be legal for them to talk to you about salaries. Definitely reach out to any recently hired veterans – this is something you might be able to find out from HR, your recruiter, or LinkedIn. Some of the things that a human being can help you with that you are less likely to get from data online is what benefits packages are offered. There's room for creativity in negotiations, but you don't want to go crazy. This will help to ground your expectations and form your counter offer.

COMPARE OFFERS

Pursue other job opportunities. Go on other job interviews. It might seem strange to do your research by going on other interviews, but it's a great way to learn what salaries are being offered in the industry. Sometimes, getting your resume past the first round is all you need to get access to some salary information from the company. This is also one of the advantages of working with a recruiting firm, as they are likely to have this information from past employees or reported by the company itself. Now, there is obviously a time commitment to this, but there are several benefits. You can practice some of the techniques throughout this book, without worry of the repercussions. If the timing is right, you might be able to use an offer from one job to ask for a better salary at another. It's also nice to have a backup offer in case the one you currently want falls through. Continuing your job search while you're negotiating can help to increase your leverage in the process.

OBSERVE

You want to be gathering information throughout the interview process, as well. Ever hear the saying in poker that you're not playing the cards, you're playing the person? The same can go for salary negotiations. Take of note of the urgency with which you are being pursued. Are there things that the interviewer notes about the position such as specific needs or concerns? These are things that you want to address throughout the interview process to demonstrate that you are the perfect candidate for the job who will solve all their problems. You also want to figure out who the decision makers for the hiring process are. You might have to understand the motivation of the boss of the person you are negotiating with, so you'll have to figure out how to help this person vouch for your case. What does a win look like to them? Do they need to hire you by a certain time? Do they have location constraints or needs that have a higher priority for being filled? Furthermore, what does the person you are going to be negotiating with respond to? Do they like hard facts and figures? Do they seem to enjoy connecting with you on a personal level? Are they tough and try to push you out of your comfort zone? All these things affect how you may respond when you counter their offer.

Whatever you find in your research will probably show you that there is a wide range in the marketplace for your services. It might be difficult to pin down an exact salary. This is a good thing. The more unknowns mean there is more leeway for you to make an argument based on all the value that you will bring to the company. Your position may have additional responsibilities, be in an especially challenging environment, have a different schedule – all sorts of things not addressed in the position, itself. As you gather your research, you want to be thinking out what makes you special for this particular position. Do you fulfill multiple requirements that other people are unlikely to fill? Do you have special certifications that the marketplace doesn't account for? All these things that are value adds are also leverage points that you can use in your negotiation. This is why doing your homework before going into a negotiation is so critical to your success.

SUMMARY
- Salary research is important to gauge the range that you can counter with that will be reasonable to the company.
- Use all resources available to you including online job sites, research reports, and your own networking.

- Understand the dynamics of your situation and the characteristics of your potential employer. Understand their needs, including the needs of the people who will be making the decision about hiring you.
- Think about what sets you apart from others in the marketplace and keep these in mind when you formulate your counter.

CHAPTER SEVEN

SETTING YOUR EXPECTATIONS AND GOALS

"Until input (thought) is linked to a goal (purpose)
there can be no intelligent accomplishment."
- Paul G. Thomas, scientist and writer

I recently helped a friend negotiate his salary, mid-career. He had been with his company for nearly a decade, had done very well with them, and just found out ahead of his performance review that he would be getting a small raise for that year. He was already highly paid for his position in this industry and unfortunately, there wasn't much precedent for paying someone at his position any higher. But after reviewing his situation, I felt that my friend should get more. This friend of mine was overworked, managing two and a half times the number of projects that his peers were, and provided outstanding work according to his latest performance review. We sat down to talk about his goals before negotiating. He felt that he deserved a higher raise for what he had been doing. After all, he was still being paid less than what it would cost the company to hire enough people to do the work he was doing. But more importantly, he just didn't want to keep the pace he was going. His salary didn't justify the amount of work he was doing. So when we went to negotiate with his managers, we brought up the compensation issue first. As we expected, they balked at paying him much higher beyond the market. But then we offered what my friend really wanted. He presented a plan that allowed some of his projects to be distributed to other members of the team, while he trained them and oversaw the projects' success. He found a way to lessen his workload, while still justifying his salary to his company. It also helped the company see how critical a member of the team my friend was, and were happy to work through this arrangement. If he went into the negotiation without this goal in mind, he might not have been happy with the results, even if he did get a raise. That's why it's important to figure out what's important to you, first.

Some might assume that your goal in a salary negotiation is to get the highest compensation possible. I would argue that your goal is actually to extract the most value. There are some important differences in that subtlety. You might value vacation days or opportunities to accelerate your career more than your base salary. As you do your market research and learn more about the company through the interview process, you will get an idea of what you can negotiate. You are unlikely to get the highest number for every point you negotiate in your compensation package. So it's important to plan to negotiate the things with the greatest priority for you.

Our next task then, is to understand value in the context for you, and for your company. It's important to understand what *you* want when it comes to your compensation. Just as how the company has a perception of your value, you must assess the value of what is being offered to you. This will help you define your goals, and figure out what you can leverage.

Understanding your BATNA

In salary negotiations, you must understand what you will minimally accept. In negotiation parlance, BATNA is your best alternative to negotiated agreement[1]. You must ask yourself, "If these negotiations fail, what options do I have?" I just think of it as the worst case scenario if the negotiations do not work out. This will help set the bottom floor of what you are willing to accept in the negotiation. This is called your reserve.

Let's say you've been searching for a job for several months. Your savings are almost used up, and you need to get a job soon to provide for your family. You haven't lined up any other interviews. If the negotiations don't work out, you're left without any other job prospects. In this case, your BATNA is quite weak. You can't negotiate too aggressively, because your alternatives are much worse than your current situation. Your reserve might be to accept the job even at a much lower salary.

Let's look at a situation where you have a stronger BATNA as a counter example. You are on terminal leave for the next two months, meaning you are still getting a paycheck from the military while you do your job search. You've gone through a few interviews already, and have a couple offers lined up that you would be willing to take. Now your position is very strong. If you don't end up negotiating an offer with the company you're interviewing with, you have other options that you would be happy with. You can leverage this position to extract more value out of the deal. Your reserve might be to accept only if the offer beats the other ones that are out there for you.

See how BATNA changes your leverage in a negotiation? If your worst case scenario isn't that big a deal to you, then you've got a strong starting position from which to work.

SO WHAT'S THEIR BATNA?

Let's flip that around. What's the company's BATNA? You need to understand their bargaining position, as well. You might have a strong BATNA, but perhaps the company does, too. If the company can't cut a deal with you, what will they do? Do they need to fill the position immediately, or can they wait several months? Can they move on to their second favorite candidate very easily? As much as you want to negotiate against this company, you have to assess how far you can push them. If their BATNA is also strong, then you have to be cautious.

WHAT'S YOUR BEST SCENARIO?

Now that you understand BATNA for you and your potential employer, it's time to set goals. Prioritize what YOU want. There might be things you will not budge on, like location, or certain healthcare benefits. What about things that are not as important to you? Perhaps you don't need a relocation bonus since you've already got the military moving you. When you assess the offer, don't get excited because it offers a bunch of benefits. Get excited if the benefits are relevant to you.

Now, your company will also have a best case scenario. Rarely will their best case align with yours. In your negotiation, you want to push toward their reserve while fulfilling your priorities. Look for things that are low on your priority that are important to the company. Perhaps you don't care where you move for work, but the company is having trouble finding talent for a certain location. If you offer to move, make sure to ask for something important to you in return.

A NOTE ON ZOPA

The intersection between your acceptable range and the company's acceptable offer is your Zone Of Possible Agreement or ZOPA[2]. This is just another fancy negotiation term. All you need to understand is that where your expectations and your employer's expectations coincide is the range of possible outcomes. Your ideal outcome is to get your concessions near the higher end of the ZOPA. In setting goals, your best case scenario is the high end of the ZOPA. Anything you'd be willing to accept falls between that and your BATNA. Why is this important? People want to negotiate with reasonable people. It's the only way to ensure a compromise can occur. Go too far in your demands, and the other party may just walk away, thinking that you are too unreasonable to persuade.

Keep in mind that while you may set your BATNA and goals before going into a negotiation, these things can change throughout the process. Perhaps another job offer comes along or you learn that the company has a dire need to hire you. Information and situations like this may arise during the process so be sure to adjust your expectations and strategies throughout. Ultimately, your success is how you define it. You are successful if you get what YOU want, not just a bunch of high numbers on your pay stub.

SUMMARY

• Success in a salary negotiation is about getting the most value for yourself.

• Define your range – BATNA, reserve, and best case scenario.

• Understand what your company will want to get out of the negotiation to determine the ZOPA.

• Prioritize the things you want as your goals. Use the things that are less important to you as leverage points.

• What you want or need will direct where you will not budge and where you can compromise in your demands.

CHAPTER EIGHT

AVOID ANSWERING THIS QUESTION

"Information is a negotiator's greatest weapon."
- Victor Kiam, entrepreneur

When you go to a car dealership and the salesperson asks you what you would like to pay for a car today, do you tell them? You shouldn't. Let's just pretend that you feel especially friendly and let the salesperson know your price range is $15,000-$20,000. What do you think will happen next? I'd be willing to bet you won't be seeing too many cars less than $20,000 that day.

In salary negotiations, pieces of information like this are extremely valuable. Employers may try to learn what your expectations are or what you previously made so that this figure can become an anchor point for your negotiations. Even though it doesn't make sense to me, it's common practice to base your salary on what you previously made, even if it has little to do with what you are being hired to do. I guess it's just the cynical side of human nature not to give someone too much of a boost up. Providing salary information cannot help you, and at best, starts you in a poor position for negotiation. Employers and recruiters know this, and will often ask early on in the process to try to find out what your prior salary was, or what you expect it to be. Understand that the only thing that giving out your previous salary or salary requirements will do is give your employer the upper hand in negotiations, or screen you out of the process for having too high of a starting point.

Neither of these are consequences you want to deal with at this point. If the job doesn't pay you enough, you aren't going to take it anyway. You want to at least get to the point where you can make an argument based on your value.

There is no law requiring you to divulge salary information. Sometimes, a company will make it a policy to request this information. So the person talking to you will say, "Aw shucks, it's our company policy, we really need you to tell us your salary." It's an easy way for them to point to "the system" as an excuse for doing something. Even then, you can usually avoid this question. I discuss how you can answer it appropriately if you have to, later on in this chapter. Many people will understand if you avoid answering this question. Some will try to jerk you around and pressure you. They'll give you a hard time and possibly even threaten that you cannot continue on in the process if you don't give this information. This should be a warning sign to you. The person or company may not be savvy with negotiations. Proceed with caution and professionalism. You could take a strong tack and tell them that this is not anything you would expect from a professional organization or that you would like to work with a different recruiter. My recommendation would be to not work for a company that bullies you during this. Remember, the interview process is as much an opportunity for you to screen the company as it is for them to screen you. Of course, not everybody has this luxury of playing hardball, so I cover at the end of the chapter how to respond if you *have* to respond.

DO NOT ANSWER THIS QUESTION IF YOU CAN AVOID IT

If you are speaking to a person and they ask you this question, there are a few ways you can defer. You should have a few of these responses ready, because they may try to ask you in several different ways:

1. "I'd like to base my salary on the value I will bring to the company, and not based on a number from my history. Let's see that we are a good fit for each other first."

2. "What is the salary being offered?" Turn the tables on them and make it seem that you need to be wooed with a competitive offer.

3. "I will not be divulging that, so let's please move on." If you're feeling cheeky, or the person asking is being pushy and can't seem to get the hint, then sometimes the direct approach is appropriate.

4. "I prefer not to divulge my salary, as I am sure your company does not expect employees to share salaries with each other." Yes, many companies include a non-disclosure policy on salaries amongst employees. Use it against them.

WHAT IF YOU HAVE TO FILL OUT AN APPLICATION THAT ASKS THIS QUESTION?

Many companies start off their recruitment process by having you fill out application forms. These forms may include questions pertaining to your salary history. You will be asked to fill out every box. Isn't it convenient that companies can avoid their most difficult tasks by outsourcing this to a software program or questionnaire? There are a few things you can do to get around this:

1. Write, "NA," or, "Flexible," or, "Will discuss in person." An answer that is non-committal would be ideal. Not all applications will let you put a non-numerical number in this box however. In this case, try number 2.

2. Ask the employer the salary range for this position, or get it from the job posting, and put the higher number. You can always negotiate this later on, saying that this number did not include some other areas of compensation that need to be included for you to move forward with the offer.

3. Get a referral so you can skip this process. Really. Sometimes, these applications can be skipped entirely if you network your way in or have someone give you a referral. Not something I want to focus on in this book, but worth researching and executing if you've got the time.

4. Put any reasonable number that you can down. There are two strategies to this. You can write the highest number that you can calculate. If you're putting down salary expectations, do the research and put down the maximum number in that range. Or, if you think

that the number will screen you out of the process, put a more reasonable expectation so that you get past it, and work on negotiating up. Just understand that you could be putting yourself in a poor starting position. A poor starting position is better than no starting position if you're hurting for a job though. If you're going to be putting down your military salary, I've got a few tips on calculating your compensation in the next section.

WHAT DID YOU MAKE IN THE MILITARY?

Taking into account all aspects of compensation, you may find that your military pay compares favorably with civilian pay for similarly skilled jobs. The difficult thing is breaking down all the things that go into military salaries. It behooves you to be able to give the highest calculation of what you previously made. Now, DO NOT LIE. Your potential employer can always find out your salary history by requesting W-2's or calling your former employer. And of course, military pay is public information. However, you will be able to explain that your TOTAL compensation is actually much higher than what you make. This is the number you want to figure out and that you want to use.

First, understand that there is not a specific number to explain your total compensation. While you could look up military pay charts, I find that they often lack information about your total compensation. Things like BAH, BAS, and hazard pay can make your salary much higher than what you see in pay charts. You also get healthcare, and a retirement fund (TSP, which is similar to a 401k), and certain bonuses for when you re-enlist. When you give a number to your employer, you generally want to give the highest number from your calculations.

What if you are a reservist, and only work part time while you're doing this job search. You only make a portion of what you would make if you were Active Duty. It's important to be honest of course, but understand what you are answering. I would say something along the lines of, "The full compensation for a person in my position is $X." If they ask you, you can walk them through the math of what a person in your position would make, full time. It is important that you are able to defend and back up all aspects of your salary. If you're being asked to fill out a form, this is the number you want to input. If you're being asked verbally, say, "My base salary was X, but including benefits, my overall compensation was in the range of Y."

The number you give isn't just your salary, but your compensation as a whole, which includes all the perks and benefits we talked about. Also notice I said previous position. Sometimes, it helps to highlight that you were in a professional position, not just "in the military," as some employers may assume. Now this is purely anecdotal on my part, but I have felt that people have a general perception that coming from the military, you are underpaid. You do not want them to maintain this idea if that is the way they think. Rather, you have developed important and relevant skills through your work and deserve to be recognized for it. Always make sure to emphasize that your job was a professional one, even if it entailed blowing stuff up.

Summary

- Avoid answering this question, if possible.
- Put a high, but reasonable, number down if you must.
- Make sure you consider the entirety of your compensation package when thinking about supplying an answer to this question.
- Do the homework to be able to support the number you provide to the employer.

CHAPTER NINE

NEGOTIATION TACTICS

"Diplomacy is the art of getting what you want,
without offending anyone too badly."
- Christopher Nuttall, from Bookworm

Salary negotiations are a bit different than other types of negotiations. You want to present yourself as principled and tough, but also fair. In the end, the negotiation fails if you don't maintain a positive feeling on both sides. You might have some flexibility in this. If you're negotiating with HR and not someone you will ultimately work with, you might be able to be a bit more aggressive. Even better, if you're working through a recruiter, you can be tougher on him to make sure he's got your best interest at heart when he's negotiating for you. Still, you want to maintain a good working relationship with everyone. This would behoove you as a professional as it is the start of your reputation and you never know who you might have to rely on, later in your career. Here are the most common negotiation techniques to understand.

BRACKETING

At some point in the negotiation process you may have to come up with a range for some number or other, such as salary, or bonus. I've talked in the previous chapter about why you don't want to be the first to give a value, but at some point, it might be unavoidable. There are a couple approaches that you can take for this. The first is providing a range. One might assume that if you give a range, the negotiations will veer toward the lower end of the scale. However, research has shown that "tandem anchoring", can yield better results in negotiating[1]. This may be because providing a range makes you seem more open to compromise, which can maintain the sort of relationship that you want in a negotiation to get things done. If you do this, I would recommend figuring out what is a reasonable midpoint, and making that your LOWER range. In effect, by including a reasonable number within your range, it makes your overall proposal seem reasonable. However, by making that the starting point, rather than the end point, you have much more room to maneuver toward the upper end of the spectrum.

FAIR OFFER

On the other hand, I've seen and experienced myself the anxiety in coming up with a range that is reasonable. Putting forth a range makes it immediately obvious that you are embarking on a negotiation. Sometimes, that in itself has a negative context. Knowing my personality and character, I like to just state what I believe to be fair. Take the range from your research and chose the high number on the scale. I like this method because it suits my personality, and it makes me come across as confident in my reasoning. Use either method to your advantage. Which brings me to the next point...

ASK FOR MORE THAN YOU EXPECT

Whatever you think is reasonable for your salary is probably an under estimate. You should ask for more than you expect because you just might get it and you increase the perceived value of your services[2]. Note that I am saying you should ask for more than YOU expect. This is because most people undervalue themselves. If, in your research, you find that there are clear salary limits in a company's compensation structure, then do not make an offer that clearly exceeds the next promotional pay scale. But keep in mind, people get stuck all the time figuring out the "right" number to counter. They hem and haw and worry about what others will think if they say something ridiculous. Don't worry about how ridiculous you think your number will be. You will not be picking it out of a vacuum. Like horseshoes and hand grenades, close is good enough. If asked, you will be able to back up why you are worth what you are asking. That's the range you should be concerned about. If you can reasonably lay out why you are worth whatever you ask, your employer can't argue your logic, although they may debate what they can provide. This is good in another respect. Since you set the expectation high, you will be negotiating down from this number. While you will still end up above the original offer, you will look like you have compromised and made concessions, making you a very agreeably person to negotiate with. It is all part of your strategy to get what you deserve, even if they don't realize it.

DON'T GIVE UP SOMETHING FOR NOTHING

Let's assume that your company asks you to concede on a point at some point in the negotiation. You had asked for a compensation package that included an increase of $8,000 in salary and $3,000 for a relocation bonus. In all honesty, you don't really care about relocation bonus because the military is covering your final move (but your employer doesn't know that), and you just wanted to throw it in as a bigger overall ask because you know that they don't give signing bonuses. You haven't gotten to talking about the salary yet, but your future employer says, "Unfortunately, we took a look at the relocation bonus and it is just not something we can offer. We see you as a top quality candidate though, and we can come up $5,000 in salary."

That's great! But that's not what you asked for. And the company has just admitted that the $5,000 that they are paying are for your talents. So they're basically asking you to give up on any relocation bonus in exchange for nothing. This is where you turn it on them. "I really appreciate that recognition of my value. But relocation bonus was something I factored into the compensation package and is really important to me and my family, as moving ourselves for this company, and that will be a significant cost to us. We've already come down $3,000 on the salary issue. I don't think it's fair for us to make this big change to support the company without something in exchange. Since you are flexible in salary, why not add $1,000 more and I will forgo the relocation bonus requirement?" See how even though you've gotten what you want, this statement makes it seem like you are conceding a great deal more? It is important to understand where value is generated in a negotiation. Starting high, as we stated previously, gives you room to work down. But every time you work down, gives you more opportunities to trade for greater value. This is why just starting the negotiation process is so powerful.

NEGOTIATING WITH A MIDDLEMAN

Your interview process may include meeting several different people. Some or all may have an impact on your salary negotiations. Or your interview may be with your future manager, who must get the contract approved by his boss and HR. Or you may be working with a recruiter who will be negotiating on your behalf. Adding more people to the negotiation complicates things to an extent. If you are negotiating with someone who is not the ultimate decision maker and they keep saying, "I'll have to run this by someone for approval," then you need to start off by understanding how to get them to be your champion. Building rapport with this person is especially important. Realize that their greatest concern may not be making you happy, but to look good for their bosses. You want to make it as easy as possible for them to do their job while supporting your cause.

IF THE PERSON IS CLEARLY ON YOUR SIDE

This is the easiest case. Everything you say and do that reinforces your value will help them justify your counter offer. You also want to work with this person to understand where the decision makers may balk or be supportive. Make this person an ally. Make sure that they follow your lead by asking questions like the following:

"Do you feel what I've said is reasonable?"

"Where do you think they will have the most issues with this?"

"What have you seen them be flexible with in the past?"

Make them feel like part of your team. Be sure to show gratitude for their assistance. "I'm glad to have the opportunity to work with people like you in this company. What would make my case stronger in your mind?" As you work with them through the process, you are, in effect, feeding them the arguments that they will take to the decision makers.

IF THE PERSON IS NEUTRAL OR AGAINST THE NEGOTIATION

Your recruiter tells you that this is unorthodox. The HR rep says that the company doesn't like to negotiate. If this person is not the decision maker, you have to get them to push past their own discomfort.

You could say, "I would really just like the opportunity to present my case. What's the most reasonable way to present this to them?" By doing this, you skip over giving them the decision whether or not to proceed.

Prod a little further with, "I don't want to walk away from this great opportunity over having a discussion about salary. I would just like them to see my counter for consideration."

A stronger approach would be, "I am enthusiastic about this opportunity, but I cannot accept under the current terms. Is the company unwilling to even consider it?"

Being more aggressive and letting them know in more concrete language can also be effective. "I will walk," or, "I cannot accept," may be the push they need if you are in a position to play hardball.

Call upon a higher authority to relinquish the decision from the middleman. "I'm really excited about this opportunity and my requests, I believe, are reasonable for the market. When I interviewed with Jim, he seemed amenable to ensuring that I got a fair compensation for this position. Would you bring this back up with him?"

Or, "I don't mean to be difficult, but this is important to me and I would like for them to at least hear my case for a counter. We ultimately both want to be happy with the compensation package. I can assure you I will be reasonable and flexible in working with the company to make it happen."

Think about what the other person needs in their position. Perhaps the HR rep doesn't want to look like they are being meek and needs to bring a good deal back to his manager. If this person is going to go to bat for you, reiterate that you will not make him look bad for doing so. Ensure that the negotiation process will be conducted professionally.

WHAT IF YOU MISSPEAK?

In general, for a salary negotiation, you want to avoid talks taking a contentious turn. If you can sense this happening, you might have to become more conciliatory. There are a few ways to handle this. First, start off by showing appreciation and reiterating that progress has been made, even if it feels like you are at an impasse.

"Thank you for putting so much effort in this. This actually makes me want to work at your company even more.

Another response could be, "I appreciate all the progress we've made so far. I don't mean to make this difficult. But I'm new to this, and this is important to me to get a fair offer."

AVOID AN IMPASSE

Move on with points that seem irreconcilable to return to later. Making progress in other areas will facilitate greater progress overall.

"It looks like this might be a difficult point. Perhaps there are other places we could compromise."

Or, "Let's return to this later on. There are a few other areas that I would like to discuss where I think we can find common ground."

IF YOU MADE AN ERROR IN COMING IN TOO LOW

Just explain why your reasoning has changed. "I had originally said that a $50,000 base salary would be acceptable to me, but now that we've received the contract, I would like to revise that number higher because there are some benefits that I'd expected that aren't a part of the compensation package."

IF YOU MADE AN ERROR IN COMING IN TOO HIGH

Concede without conceding anything. "I can understand why the number I presented may be hard for you to reach. But I really want to agree on something we can both be happy with. Just understand that I'm flexible."

Ultimately, mistakes happen, but until they are set in a contract that you have signed, you can smooth it over. Don't try to hide your mistakes. Admit that they happened and explain why you'd like to adjust. Retain the air of professionalism and your requests will seem reasonable. And if it's not a dire point to you, you can always just decide to move on to negotiate more important points to you.

CLOSING – DON'T FORGET TO SHUT UP

Of all the techniques mentioned in this chapter, this one might be the most important and most difficult. At any point in the negotiation, you will have laid out your explanations and then end with an offer put to your employer. For example, "I will be moving my family from across the country to take on this important and tough to fill position. The move will incur a cost, but I can ensure that it will be done within a reasonable range. Will the company be able to cover up to $3,000 in relocation expenses?"

Whenever you've laid out an offer like this, the next thing you should do is SHUT UP. Don't think that once the question is out there, and there is no response, you can convince someone by "adding" more logic to it. Sometimes, you forget a point or two. Don't worry about it. The silence may take up minutes. Doesn't matter. If they have a question, they will ask. If they say no, you will ask why and have an opportunity to follow up. At this point, adding anything after you've put out "the ask" makes it seem like you are wavering. I cannot emphasize this enough. Once you ask for something, SHUT UP.

ASK FOR JUST A BIT MORE

Let's say you're near the end of negotiations. You might have the opportunity to ask for just a bit more. The HR rep says, "Our best offer includes an extra week of unpaid vacation time."

You might think, great! The salary is already better than I expected, and now I have more vacation days than I will ever take. This is not how you want to respond however. Instead, you'd want to say, "Starting salary is a much more significant issue for me, but I understand that you have done your best to make a fair offer. If I'm going to have to trade *unpaid* vacation days for salary, then I think it is reasonable to expect two weeks of vacation time, rather than one."

Or you could say, "I can let go of the salary issue, but unpaid vacation time isn't really acceptable. Could you make it a paid vacation instead?" You might think to yourself that this is you being unreasonable. Just be sure to use this technique *at the end* of your negotiations. Understand that people are more amicable to fulfilling requests when they have just previously filled one. This is why charities keep hitting you up immediately after a donation to try to get you to sign up for just one more month or give just a few dollars more to reach their goal. Your employer will not want to lose you for one last, small point. The big portions have been hammered out, now get your last dig in. You might think that this is being petty, but I assure you that if you get what you ask for, you will work for every bit of it at your job. The opposite won't be true. If you don't negotiate for it now, the company is not going to come back to offer it to you later on.

SUMMARY

- Give a figure that works to your advantage, whether you bracket or provide a fixed point.
- When you are offered a compromise, see if you can use it to leverage other points of the negotiation.
- Don't give things away for free.
- Be conciliatory…when you have to be.
- Ask. And then shut it.

CHAPTER TEN

WHAT TO DO WHEN YOU GET AN OFFER

*"If I advocate cautious optimism it is not because I do not have faith
in the future but because I do not want to encourage blind faith."*
- Aung San Suu Kyi

Congratulations! If you've received an offer from a potential
employer, you are now in an ideal situation to negotiate. What this
means is that if you accept, you will soon become an employee of the
company. Pending your acceptance of the contract, you now know
that the employer wants you to work for them. DO <u>NOT</u> ACCEPT.
If you can avoid it, and I can't think of any common situation why
you couldn't, never accept an offer immediately. I don't care how
good of an offer it is. You might be thinking, "But the offer is TEN
times better than I expected. Why shouldn't I take it?" Let me count
the ways:

1. Generally, this offer is a verbal one. You might be concerned that
an employer could rescind it, but that would be in poor taste, and in
some places, illegal (although it would be difficult to prove before
you get lawyer happy). So the kind of company that would retract a
verbal offer is not one that you would want to work for, anyway. Rest
assured, the offer is not going to go away or get worse. Conversely, if
you accept the offer at this point, even if just verbally, you are pretty
much bound to it. So you do not want your emotions to cloud your
judgment and bind you to something that may not be optimal.

2. You need time to evaluate. Even if this is a great offer, you have to understand that this is the first offer. The first offer is rarely the best offer that the employer is giving. Furthermore, compensation packages can be complex and include things like insurance, expense accounts, retirement plans, and vacation/sick days. You need to review these and consider the package as a whole.

3. Taking some time and playing it cool is a high leverage sort of move. In any negotiation, if you accept too quickly, it'll make the other side question the value of their offer. They'll either think, "Dang, I could have gotten a better deal," or, "Maybe what I'm getting isn't actually worth what I think it is." Don't give them the opportunity to get near this line of thinking about you.

4. You need time to strategize a counter. The first offer is probably what they give everybody. It's what they are used to doing. The company might not be valuing YOU properly. You have to assess what they missed and how you can persuade them to give you what you deserve. You have to consider if the offer is good relative not just to your own desires, but also within the industry, location, and company.

It is important to understand that this is a very tenuous position for the employer. Up until this point, they've pretty much had all the leverage. But now they've spent the time and money to recruit you and have decided you are the one they want. If you walk away, it could be quite the waste of resources for them. If you've done a good job interviewing and demonstrating value, they might even have a subconscious fear of missing out on attracting you as a candidate after all that effort. This is great, because even if there are many other possible candidates, they would rather not miss out on you. You don't want to have done all the work up to this point and offend them, so your next words are very important. Don't get cute with it. What you want to do is defer some time to think about the offer, but make it clear that you are still very interested.

Start by saying, "Thank you for this opportunity. I've been impressed and excited about working for your company throughout this process. I appreciate your offer and would like the time to go over it with my family." I don't care if you live alone, using family as a reason for taking some time to consider applies to everyone – wouldn't your mom appreciate it if you considered her in this decision?

Another response could be, "I was really hoping for an offer from your company and am thrilled to have this opportunity to consider. As you know, I have several options to consider and will be doing my due diligence to compare all offers. Will there be any flexibility in yours?" Only use this if the company know your interviewing for other positions and is OK with it (for example, they found you at a hiring conference or through a recruiting firm). Notice that the statement starts off extremely enthusiastic. That second sentence is the important one though. You're dropping a hint that your talents could very easily be taken elsewhere but you're not doing it because of spite. You're just doing the logical thing. The last question is also important. You cannot assume that the person across the table will get the hint or will even think to reconsider at this point. This is the time to ask. It's a sort of soft close.

You can also ask, "When do I need to respond to your offer?" If you know you've been doing well throughout the process, you can just do the cool thing and be straightforward with it. You're not even asking if you can take the time to go over it. You're assuming you can and need to know when the deadline is. This one's a bit bolder than the aforementioned statements.

Your employer might balk a bit. So reassure them. You don't want them to walk away at this point because they think you are uninterested or will not budge. So make small, small, small concessions at this point. Even better, make them think you're making concessions.

"I can see you want to move quickly with this, and I want to support that and start on the right foot. I was thinking a week, but I could give an answer in three days." You weren't thinking a week, but they will think you were now. Three days sounds like a deal!

"I hope I'm not being difficult. But this is my first compensation review after the military. It behooves me to do my homework, don't you think?" Yes, blame it on being from the military. They can't fault you for defending America these past few years.

Finally, if an employer is really pressuring you to accept the offer, I would be wary. It would not be the most professional thing to do and I would be concerned if this is their response.

ONE CAVEAT

I understand that not everyone has the luxury of potentially losing a job offer. This is why I talk about priorities earlier in this book. There are a lot of things that go into why you should take a job. Do you need to put food on the table for your family, right now? Is this the only job offer you've had in months of trying? Are you in a highly competitive market and this is your only chance? Is this job acceptable to you, even with this low compensation? If your priority at this point might be to have a job first, salary be damned. In this case, go ahead and accept. But that doesn't mean you are out of luck. You can do the following to ensure that you have the job, while giving you at least some opportunity to get a better offer.

"Thank you for your offer. I am writing to accept. I would also like to ask you some questions about the salary. In my research, a qualified person for this position, of which I surpass, would make $5,000 more. I do not say this as in anyway meaning that I do not accept this offer. In fact, I accept regardless of whether you have room for flexibility or not. However, I was wondering if you have flexibility in the matter and to consider it, with my demonstrated commitment and enthusiasm. If not, I would be interested in proposing an accelerated timeline for review."

In taking this position, you are much safer in ensuring that you have the job, while giving you room to move up. Here, you are giving yourself much less leverage than you would if you negotiated beforehand, but that's understandable because you are in a position with low leverage. No worries. Do great at this job and try negotiating later on or give yourself an opportunity to move to a better position. Sometimes, you have to negotiate with life before you negotiate with your employer.

SUMMARY

- DO NOT ACCEPT THEIR FIRST OFFER. Defer for more time to respond.
- Be gracious and professional.
- Reiterate your interest and your fit for the job.
- Remember your goals. If you have to take a less than ideal offer that still meets your expectations, then do it.

CHAPTER ELEVEN

MANAGING YOUR COUNTER

'How "extreme" should a first offer be?
"Just this side of crazy"'
- Margaret Neale, Management Professor, Stanford

Although I'm putting this chapter here, at the end of the book, a counter can take place anywhere along the process. Just realize that whenever you propose something different to what has been offered, you are making some sort of counter. Whatever their expectations were, you are proposing to do something that more adequately benefits you.

WHAT IS A COUNTER?
The strategy for your counter is essentially explaining:

1. That offer won't work for me.
2. Here's what would work for me.
3. This is why.

There is, of course, a wide range of things that you can do to communicate in between those three statements. As a professional, you'll have to do it in a way that works in your favor. To increase your likelihood of success in a salary negotiation, you are essentially explaining:

1. That won't work for me, but that's OK because I have a solution that will work to both our benefit.
2. Here's what would work for me, and it should be considered very reasonable and fair to both of us.
3. This is why, and it's based on a fair exchange of value between you and I.

Here's how you do it.

START WITH THEIR PERSPECTIVE

When you counter, you're basically disagreeing with their valuation of you for the position. How do you disagree without coming across as a jerk? Your success likely depends on getting the other person on your side.

Understand where they are at with you. This is a tenuous position for the employer. Once negotiations begin, one of their considerations must be whether or not they can convince you to accept or if you will walk away. You need to be just on the edge of them thinking you want to walk.

"Thank you for this offer. I am enthusiastic about joining your company. There are just a few areas of the contract that I would like to discuss before moving forward."

You can also soften your counter with, "I would really like to join the company. It's hard for me to accept when comparable offers for this position are higher."

Think about this from their position as a reasonable person. They want to hire you. They want to make you happy so that you will be happy working for them. They don't want to waste their time in case they need to move on from you. They don't know what you want. They might not understand the value that you bring. This would be a good time to hint at that information.

"This company is number one on my list. I've received offers that are higher than what you are offering. If we can close that gap, I would definitely join your company."

You could also say, "I am really happy about this offer and am looking forward to taking on the challenges of this position. After reviewing, I had some questions about the contract. Before moving forward and accepting, I want to work with you to see if the company would be open to addressing some areas of concern for me."

Let them know that you are happy with the company and that you are *willing* to join, as soon as you both come to a fair and equitable agreement.

REINFORCE VALUE

At this point in the negotiation, remind them of why you are worth the extra pay. It doesn't matter if it's your dream job or an entry level position. You have unique qualities that set you apart from other candidates. This is what justifies your counter.

Start with, "I am glad to have this opportunity to take on this role. In reviewing the job requirements, there are skills and experiences that I bring that were preferred but not required by the candidate. I don't think this is reflected in the offer and would like to work with you to see if there is room to bring it closer to market rate."

You might also say, "I understand it may be difficult to negotiate the starting salary because this is an entry level position. My background leading teams in this environment has demonstrated that I am a fast learner and will mesh with your company quickly. Can we look at shortening the review period so that I can be evaluated earlier in my career for potential promotion?"

Justify by using *their* perception of value. It doesn't matter if you've got more years of experience, a great degree, or extra skills that will make you a rock star at this job. If these things don't equate to their bottom line, they can't justify giving you more money. You might guarantee that you can show up to work on time every day, but there's little value in this. The employer expects this already. Instead, think of the problems that the company needs to solve and why what you bring is critical.

TRADE ON VALUE

Value isn't always about what you bring to the position. If at this point you have several offers for similar positions, you could use this as a way of demonstrating value. "I'm fielding different offers at this point. While I like this company the best, I am getting offered $2,000 more with the other employer. Would you consider matching that?"

Or, "The fair market range from my research shows that this position makes in the $60,000 range. I would like to discuss a higher salary for bringing me on that is more in line with the market."

TRADING ON THE VALUE OF DIFFERENT ITEMS IN THE CONTRACT

Sometimes, a company cannot give you a raise, but they do have room to give you a bonus. Understanding the nuances of the hiring budget can create significant leverage. "I would love to join the team to start tackling some of the challenges we talked about. As we've also discussed, taking on this job would mean some significant changes for my family and I. I understand that the salary is non-negotiable, but I think it would be fair to consider a one-time reimbursement or bonus to cover moving and relocation costs."

You can also get more specific. "I understand that you are not able to budge on salary, but there are several expenses that I will be taking on to fill this position. Would the company be willing to share in providing these expenses to bring me on? I could even look at choosing a more basic healthcare plan to save the company if you could offer a stipend to cover some supplies."

COUNTER-COUNTERS

Now, even with your great explanation, the company may counter you again, or flat out say no, or offer something completely different. Keep in mind negotiations are flexible. There is no strict timeline or maximum number of times either of you can counter. If the company is willing to work with you, take this as a positive sign. Manage this tension judiciously. Too much tension and you could lose the offer. Keep working and collaborating until you have a deal that is acceptable to you.

This is why it is important to understand your goals and minimums before you go into negotiations. You have as much right to say no as they do. If they won't budge and their offer doesn't meet your BATNA, no hard feelings. Walk away knowing that you haven't accepted less than you deserve.

If you do negotiate something better but you don't reach every single one of your goals, that's OK, as well. You have gotten more value by merely negotiating than if you had not at all. This is how you get what you deserve.

SUMMARY

- When you're about to counter think of their position. Address their concerns and reassure that you would accept a fair offer for you.
- Collaborate with the recruiter to figure out what is flexible in the offer and where you can trade value.
- Counter by exchanging *value*. Frame your counter with how your position is more reasonable.
- Evaluate success through the lens of your goals.

CHAPTER TWELVE

ACCEPTING THE OFFER

"Therefore the clever combatant imposes his will on the enemy, but does not allow the enemy's will to be imposed on him."
- Sun Tzu

One day, out of the blue, my new manager gave me a call. He wanted to rework my contract. He was doing this for all the employees after he took over for my previous boss. "We're giving all the employees at your level $10,000 bonus in recognition of your contributions." I was pretty excited. He said he would send over the new contract to read over and if I could just get it back to him as soon as possible. I couldn't open the e-mail attachment fast enough when I got it. There, in writing, was the $10,000 bonus. As I read further along however, I grew concerned. The bonus would only vest after three years, meaning, if I left the company before then, I would have to pay it back. For the job I was working, $10,000 over three years was not comparable to the raises I would be expecting on my old contract. The company could release me at any time, for any reason. This was different from my current contract, which required a lay-off, or non-performance of duties. And finally, this contract added a non-compete clause. If I left or was fired, I couldn't work in the same industry in the same area for one year. None of these things were mentioned in the phone call, and I went from being elated, to being pissed. I found out later that there had been some sort of political power struggle that caused my old boss to leave. The new management was trying to shore up all the commitments from the recent hires that my old boss had made. It wasn't really a bonus. It was the smallest carrot they thought they could dangle to get us all to stay on their terms. Needless to say, many of us refused to sign the new contract. It's not so much that the bonus was inadequate. But when your new boss tries to get one by you, you immediately become wary. That's why it's so important to be careful when accepting offers.

Your success comes from taking actions that are within your control and not leaving them to chance. If you've gotten to the point in the salary negotiation that you get an offer, you're probably congratulating yourself. You've negotiated your salary and your about to accept a great offer! What could go wrong? Well, after you've successfully negotiated your starting salary your job is not done. People will often complain that "the system" is broken and the universe conspires against them. This is a defeatist attitude. The system is run by humans, and humans are fallible. Whether conscious or accidental, people can and will falter, sometimes to your detriment. I wrote this chapter to remind you of this and to provide some things that you can do to impose *your* will, and not let the system screw you over. Let's not leave anything in the process to chance when it is possible for you to have some control over it. Best not to let anything to ruin all the great work you've done up to this point.

HOW TO SAY YES

Don't <u>say</u> yes. Huh? You don't actually accept an offer until you've signed the contract. Even once all parties have agreed to all terms, you should ask for when you will see the written contract. Your employer may want a verbal commitment from you. They probably want some sort of reassurance in good faith that after putting all this work in recruiting you, that you are not going to walk away or use this offer to play off another. Although, or because, this is non-binding, be generous in reassuring them that you will be accepting...you're just waiting to sign on the dotted line. Be enthusiastic (don't let them have any doubts), but don't let them think that their work is done. Let them know, "I'm glad we got this done and I'm excited to be joining the team. I'm ready to sign once I get a revised contract with all the changes we discussed," or simply, "Great! When I can expect to see the revised contract?"

WHAT TO KEEP TRACK OF

Many things are discussed during a salary negotiation. You don't want any terms to be left off the contract or for it to be lost in translation. Be proactive in preventing this throughout the process. Keep track of anything that is agreed upon. Make sure that you've taken notes throughout the process and written down what the terms MEAN TO YOU. If there is any room for interpretation or if you are confused, try to ask before a final contract is drafted. It takes time and effort to put together a contract, and you don't want to prolong the process after your employer has made any changes. While not necessarily critical, you don't want these talks to go on and on as it can leave people with a bad taste in their mouths or just provide more room for error.

WHAT IF THE BUSINESS DOESN'T HAVE A CONTRACT?

Employment contracts are not a requirement. If it's a small business, a startup, or a job that doesn't warrant that sort of paper work, then at this point, all you have left to do is evaluate the offer, and decide whether or not to accept. I would still suggest doing the aforementioned things of being enthusiastic and gracious in accepting and keeping track of the terms of this handshake agreement. It might also be worth doing some research on your rights in your state.

HOW TO BE PROACTIVE

Take the initiative to follow up on your own and before they send you the updated offer. You get to ensure that everyone understands *your* terms. Here's a sample:

Hello Bill,

Thank you for working with me on coming to terms on a fair compensation package. I am excited to start working with ACME Corp. I've summed up our agreements below for your review in updating the contract. Looking forward to signing on soon.

- Agreed upon base salary is $75,000.
- Unpaid vacation time can be rolled over each year, with an additional week of paid vacation up to four weeks.
- Relocation bonus will be provided up to $2,000. Expenses will be approved with receipts through HR.

- All other terms remain the same.
Please let me know if there are any questions.

Thank you,
Sign your name

Carbon copy all relevant parties. Relevant parties include the representative in HR drafting your contract, the person you negotiated with, and perhaps your manager, if he is interested in seeing how the contract talks are progressing.

GET CONFIRMATION!

You want to make sure any agreements are at least made in e-mail and acknowledged by the recipient. In some e-mail programs, you can include a read receipt that alerts you when the receiving parties open your e-mail. I would prefer to ask for an acknowledgement. If they don't respond, follow up after a reasonable amount of time with an e-mail asking about the status and confirming that all points have been approved. You want to do this because even if no new contract is drafted, this correspondence can be used as proof of all the points that were discussed. It is also possible that not all aspects of the agreed upon points will make it into the contract. Perhaps you negotiated permission from your boss to work from home. She does not intend to make this a provision in your contract, but in essence, you have approval. You want to make sure you have this in your records in case this becomes an issue in the future. This is less than preferable than getting this in your contract, but for minor issues, I would accept it and move on.

WHY ALL THE FUSS?

Keeping everything in writing is important because the people you are negotiating with may not be the people you work with, later on. The HR rep may leave the company, your manager could be fired, and your recruiter may completely forget who you are. You need to have something to refer to with your employer. Your contract and correspondence with acknowledgement from all the parties of the company are your only proof.

Once you receive the contract, go over it and make sure there is nothing unclear or that anything has changed from what you originally agreed upon. DO NOT JUST SIGN IT. If there is any doubt, be sure to ask and clarify. I would be wary of any company that tries to get you to sign or agree without a final check. Once again, all clarification should be confirmed in writing, such as e-mail. Make sure that you understand what you are required to do, as well. This can include the requirements and responsibilities of the job position, but also what aspects of the contract are subject to your performance. You don't want to realize two years into the job that you do not accrue vacation time until after three years in your position. While something like this may seem obvious, I can assure you that many first time salary negotiators, including myself, miss things like this.

And finally, when you accept, don't forget the importance of grace. "Thank you for this offer. I am excited to be working with you. I'm looking forward to what comes next in the process." Little things like this are a mark of your professionalism and go a long way toward building good will toward you with your new company and everyone that you interact with.

WHAT IF THE COMPANY ASKS YOU TO START BEFORE YOU GET THE NEW CONTRACT?

This may seem like a strange request, but I've had it happen to my peers, so a word of caution here. My friend signed on with a company. His manager guaranteed him some bonuses. My friend started training for the job and that hiring manager was let go. It took my friend another nine months of going back and forth with HR, showing the e-mails of these commitments, before he finally got those bonuses. I wouldn't recommend starting a job until the contract is in place. If you go to work for the President of the United States or this is a once in a lifetime opportunity like that, I'd say fine, let it go. In all other situations, be wary.

SUMMARY

- Get everything confirmed in writing, even if it is just an e-mail.
- Understand all aspects of what you are agreeing to, before you sign the contract.
- Be polite and accept graciously.
- Keep things in writing and follow-up on correspondence for confirmation.

CONCLUSION

NOW WHAT?

"Negotiation is not a policy. It's a technique. It's something you use when it's to your advantage, and something that you don't use when it's not to your advantage."
- John Bolton, U.S. Ambassador

I recently worked on a salary negotiation with a friend. We went back and forth with his manager, then his VP, then with HR. Ultimately, the company's policies were predicated on only giving salary increases for specific positions at particular times of the year. Our timing was just off. In the end, my friend wasn't willing to walk away or leverage his position by seeking opportunities elsewhere. So as far as the negotiation goes, it was a bust. However, he did it professionally and reasonably. He didn't get fired. Come his next performance review, he got the largest raise he'd ever received. In going through the negotiation process, he got to show the value that he was providing the company. And although the negotiation failed the first time, it ended up being successful in the end.

WIN THE WAR, NOT THE BATTLE

I'm tired of people not getting what they deserve. I'm even more tired of seeing people being unhappy about not getting what they deserve, having done nothing about it. There are two things to remember as a veteran. First, people won't just give you things. You are not entitled to it. Even after all you've sacrificed, the private sector will not hesitate to leave you on the side of the road and pass you by. This is the unfortunate reality. Secondly, you DO have a great deal of value, but YOU have to convey it. Your ability to communicate as a professional can be the difference maker in developing a high earning career.

Continue to develop these skills even after you've successfully negotiated your first job offer. Understand that there are no guaranteed results. You can only put forth your efforts in the actions that will set you up for success. So work hard, do well, and negotiate. Take action in the areas that you can control. This will be important throughout your career.

Leaving the military is a unique transition. I haven't found anything since in my career as meaningful as the time I spent serving alongside the men and women that defend this country. Despite that sense of loss, I know it was the right decision for me. My calling now is to do my best with the life that I have due to the continued sacrifices of the people serving today. It would be disrespectful if I didn't make the most of it. That's why I continue to fight for veterans to make the most of the opportunities they have earned. I hope this book gives you the tools to do just that.

Fair winds, following seas, and semper fi.

And don't forget to ask for a raise or two down the line.

ENDNOTES

Introduction: Why Do You Need This Book?

1. CareerBuilder, "Nearly One-Third of Employers Willing to Negotiate Salary Increases for Current Employees for 2011," November 10, 2010, accessed October 15, 2015, http://snip.ly/3Amn.

2. Robert W. Goldfarb, "Veterans Battle for Jobs on the Home Front," *The New York Times*, May 9, accessed November 19, 2015, http://www.nytimes.com/2015/05/10/jobs/veterans-battle-for-jobs-on-the-home-front.html.

Chapter One: Why Negotiate Your Salary?

1. CareerBuilder, "Forty-Nine Percent of Workers Do Not Negotiate Job Offers, Finds CareerBuilder Compensation Survey," August 21, 2013, accessed October 15, 2015, http://snip.ly/oJIS.

2. Aaron Gouveia, "Why Americans are Too Scared to Negotiate Salary," Salary.com, accessed October 15, 2015, http://snip.ly/e8Jq.

3. "Why Are Workers Afraid to Negotiate Salary?" Salary.com, accessed October 15, 2015, http://snip.ly/pFa7.

4. Linda Babcock and Sara Laschever, "Women Don't Ask: Negotiation and the Gender Divide," accessed October 15, 2015, http://snip.ly/mbVm.

5. Steven D. Levitt and Stephen J. Dubner, *Freakonomics: A Rogue Economist Explores the Hidden Side of Everything* (New York: HarperCollins, 2009), 5-8.

6. Camille Sweeney and Josh Gosfield, "49% of Job Candidate Never Negotiate an Initial Employment Offer. Do You?" *Fast Company*, November 11, 2013, accessed October 15, 2015, http://snip.ly/nEHm.

Chapter Three: Mindset For Success

1. Josh Bersin, "Corporate Recruiting Explodes: A New Breed Of Service Providers," Forbes, May 23, 2013, accessed November 4, 2015, http://www.forbes.com/sites/joshbersin/2013/05/23/corporate-recruitment-transformed-new-breed-of-service-providers.

2. Adam Lewis, "There Are 4 Million U.S. Job Openings: Why Are The Positions Unfilled?" Forbes, May 31, 2013, accessed October 15, 2015, http://www.forbes.com/sites/realspin/2013/05/31/there-are-4-million-u-s-job-openings-why-are-the-positions-unfilled.

3. CareerBuilder, "Forty-Nine Percent of Workers Do Not Negotiate Job Offers, Finds CareerBuilder Compensation Survey," August 21, 2013, accessed October 15, 2015, http://snip.ly/oJIS.

Chapter Seven: Setting Your Expectations And Goals

1. Brad Spangler, "Best Alternative To Negotiated Agreement (BATNA)," July 2012, accessed November 4, 2015, http://snip.ly/tdDF.

2. Brad Spangler and Heidi Burgess, "Zone Of Possible Agreement (ZOPA)," June 2013, accessed November 4, 2015, http://snip.ly/wgQq.

Chapter Nine: Negotiation Tactics

1. Daniel R. Ames and Malia F. Mason, "Tandem anchoring: Informational and politeness effects of range and offers in social exchange," *Journal of Personality and Social Psychology*, *108*, 254-274.

2. Roger Dawson, *Secrets of Power Negotiating, 15th Anniversary Edition: Inside Secrets from a Master Negotiator* (New Jersey: The Career Press, 2011), 18.

ACKNOWLEDGEMENTS

Thank you to Tom Morkes (TomMorkes.com) and the Publishers' Empire group for the feedback and support to get my butt in gear to finish this book. My gratitude for editing the manuscript and designing the cover goes to the amazing team at Publish My Book Today (Publishmybook.today). There were several people who reviewed the first drafts of the manuscript and provided direction in marketing. I greatly appreciated being able to pick your brains. Any missteps in execution were completely of my own doing.

To the men and women who served and who are still serving, I am forever in your debt. You continue to amaze, motivate, and inspire me. Thank you for your self sacrifice.

ABOUT THE AUTHOR

Byron Y. Chen was born in Lincoln, Nebraska, and grew up in Edison, New Jersey. He graduated from the United States Naval Academy in Annapolis, Maryland, and served as an officer in the United States Marine Corps. His six years of active duty included a deployment to Iraq, multiple company commands, and a tour at the prestigious Marine Corps Recruit Depot in San Diego. After leaving the military, Byron drew on his lessons in management, team building, and problem solving in high pressure environments to consult with entrepreneurs on business development, marketing, and sales. He also helps companies with recruiting talented veterans to their workforce. He is actively involved in supporting veterans' causes and provides resources to service members on his blog, SuccessVets.com, with articles, videos, and podcasts.

Made in the USA
San Bernardino, CA
07 February 2016